WILDERNESS KITCHEN

A GUIDE FOR TURNING WILD GAME INTO EVERYDAY MEALS

DANIELLE HINTON
with MICHAEL ELWELL

TABLE OF CONTENTS

INTRODUCTION

By Danielle Hinton

Growing up, cooking was a huge part of my life. I spent many days with my grandma making cookies and pastries, spent Sunday evenings helping my parents cook our family's traditional Sunday roast and even spent countless hours trying to create my own concoctions (while getting in trouble for wasting ingredients on the concoctions that didn't work out). I was raised with a love of cooking and food in general.

In 2010, I met my boyfriend Michael. Michael comes from a family of hunters and grew up hunting all over Washington. As we began dating and eventually started living together, I was presented with the challenge of adapting my cooking skills to prepare all the wild game he was bringing home. Challenge accepted.

I've heard many people tell me they dislike wild game, usually because it tastes too gamey or it's too tough and I can tell you, I've definitely experienced that as well. When not field dressed, butchered, and prepared correctly, wild game can be tough to stomach. However, with Michael's experience in field dressing and butchering, and my methods for preparing and cooking, we can help you make delicious meals using your wild game that you and your family will love.

Also, If you don't have a particular type of game in your freezer, all the recipes in this book can be made with a store bought alternative. You can substitute beef for venison and elk, pork for bear, domestic turkey or chicken for wild turkey, and pork sausage for game sausage. Just make sure to cook to a safe temperature for whatever type of meat you are using (you can purchase a meat thermometer that has the cooking temperatures listed on it). You can also use most ground wild game interchangeably in these recipes.

This cookbook was created to help people make delicious, every day meals using their wild game, and to help people realize that wild game doesn't have to be intimidating or difficult to cook. I've arranged the recipes by the most common cuts of meat for ease in choosing what you want to eat for that particular meal. If organized properly in your freezer you will be able to look at your box of ground, roasts or steaks and have several recipes for each to choose from. I hope you enjoy all the recipes in this collection and find a love for wild game like I did.

Dani

FROM FIELD TO FREEZER

By Michael Elwell

Great tasting wild game starts well before you ever leave for your hunt. Having the proper tools and gear coupled with the knowledge and confidence of field dressing an animal are critical components to ensuring your meat is processed safely, cleanly and as quickly as possible. Outside of an animal's diet and their overall health when you harvest them, there are several things that can affect the quality of the meat (think tenderness and flavor) that a hunter can try to control. People often speak of the "gamey" flavor associated with wild meat and how that turns them away from eating it. In addition to following the recipes found in this cookbook, there are a few key things that you need to employ while in the field that will greatly reduce this all too common gamey flavor that may potentially plague your meat. This section is devoted to helping mitigate those issues as well as reduce the chance of losing any meat to spoiling or bone sour. If you've ever consumed wild meat that tasted gamey, there's no doubt that it was handled improperly in the field, it wasn't cooked correctly or, most likely, a combination of both. With that being said, the purpose of this portion of the book is to share my experiences with meat care in the field and to help give you, the hunter, some key principles and guidelines to effectively get your bounty from the field to your freezer.

Having the Proper Tools and Gear

Assembling a proper "kill kit" is something you should be doing in the offseason before you head out on your hunt. A kill kit is something you will always be carrying in your pack while in the field and the contents of which can vary slightly depending on what and where you're hunting. My kill kit consists of the following items; a knife with a replaceable scalpel type blade, game bags, 25 feet of 550 paracord, some orange surveyors tape to mark blood trails and a folded up sheet of Tyvek or similar drop cloth. All of this is stuffed into a little sack and I don't touch it or remove it from my pack until I get an animal down. When choosing a replaceable blade knife, I would highly recommend getting something with a blaze orange, hi-vis handle. You'd be surprised how easy it is to lose a misplaced knife when quartering an animal and the last thing you want is an exposed razor blade laying somewhere around you when you're alone a couple miles from the truck. If you use a fixed blade knife then you will obviously want to include a sharpener in your kit as well because the hide and fat of a big game animal will dull your blade faster than concrete, or so it seems. As far as selecting the best game bags, there are several good brands on the market to choose from and I will leave that to you to determine what brand will best suit your needs. Just make sure to choose the proper size bag for what you're hunting (any decent game bag company will have the size labeled with what animals they recommend them for) but as a rule of thumb, when in doubt, go bigger. Think breathability and durability when selecting these bags. Another thing you need to get squared away beforehand is a solid cooler setup. When you're hunting bear in August and deer/elk in September, you'll want to have a good cooler pre-loaded with ice and ready to go at your truck. A warm or room temperature cooler will melt your ice fairly quickly until it gets to cooling temperature so pre-cooling it at home beforehand with ice that you won't be taking with you is a good way to pro-long the life of the ice that you will be taking with you. This isn't as much of problem for a day hunt within an hour of home, assuming you can get your meat to a refrigerator or meat locker fairly quickly, but when taking a cooler with you on a multiple day trip or over a week then I always pre-cool. Just throwing a couple bags of ice in the cooler will certainly cool your meat but it will also quickly lead to a couple inches of water pooling in the bottom. Take a couple gallon water jugs and fill them ¾ of the way then throw them in your freezer at home for at least a few days beforehand. Leaving space in the jug for the water to expand when freezing will make it so the ice doesn't break the jug and then leak the water into the cooler after it melts. Placing the meat on top of the gallon jugs within the cooler will keep the quarters off the bottom and will promote more airflow around the meat. Also, make sure your cooler is clean before you head out on your hunt. Introducing bacteria laden meat with a bunch of bacteria that's already coating the inside of your cooler is a recipe for disaster. I like to clean the inside of my dry cooler with disinfecting wipes before my hunts. When considering the size of a cooler I would go with a minimum of 100 quarts for deer, black bear and antelope and 150 quarts for a boned-out elk. Throwing a sleeping bag over top your cooler full of ice that's underneath a canopy topper in the bed of your truck will keep the ice frozen for at least 7 days in the heat of late Summer. The combination of keeping direct sunlight off the cooler with the canopy topper and maximizing insulation with the sleeping bag over top is a great trick to keep that ice frozen for prolonged periods. There is obviously plenty of other gear you will need in order to get your tag filled, but as far as getting your meat taken care of in the field, just remember to assemble a reliable kill kit and get a good, clean cooler that's big enough to fit your entire quartered animal.

Weather Related Factors Affecting Finished Meat Quality

Heat and moisture are the two main things you need to worry about after you get an animal down. This unforgiving duo will allow bacteria to thrive which may lead to your meat spoiling at hyper speed. Generally, the ideal environment for bacteria is between 40 °F and 140 °F. Add some moisture to this temperature range and you're looking at bacteria growth on steroids. Getting the temperature of the meat outside of these parameters as soon as you can will help immensely with the final flavor once you go to cook it. The first thing you want to do after tagging your animal will be to get the hide off, get it quartered and get air circulating around the meat as soon as possible before placing it into your cooler. This will allow heat to rapidly dissipate. Even just a light breeze blowing around the exposed meat in a shaded area does wonders in these first stages of field care. The key word there is shaded. If you can get the meat hanging in the shade above a flowing creek then you're pretty much golden. Locating a flowing creek in the bottom of a drainage is akin to turning the AC on in your house on a 90 degree Summer afternoon. It truly is a night and day difference. The hide of an animal is an extremely thick, tough and insulating organ. Taking the hide off the meat immediately and placing it in a quality, breathable game bag not only gets the meat cooling and gets air circulating around it but the game bags also help to keep the bugs off which reduces the chance of them laying larvae in your meat. Yes, maggots may potentially infest your meat if not properly combatted. This is equally disgusting as it is completely probable without good game bags. Leaving the hide on your animal in the early season will without a doubt lead to considerable or complete bone sour and loss of meat. Bone sour is when your meat essentially rots from the inside out. The amount of heat that is stored within the center of the largest portions of an animal's quarters is truly impressive. On the back hams of an elk for instance, the outside of the skinned quarter may be cool to the touch after a few hours but the meat inside the leg around the ball joint can still be 80+ degrees. That meat will spoil to bone sour if not properly cared for. If you need to cut the leg open a bit once it's quartered to expose that major femur bone and ball joint to some air then that is exactly what you should do. If you shoot a bull elk in the evening and the temps are supposed to drop into the high 30's that night then this may not be as big of a deal as the temps are already starting to cool once you've killed it. But if you shoot this same bull in the morning and the high that day is calling for 70+ degrees and you're trying to cool the meat with the entire day ahead of you, then cut that leg open, stick it in a game bag and get it hanging in the shade. Again, next to a creek if at all possible. (fig. 1) In general, it's not difficult to cool the meat when hunting in the West from about the second week of October onward. At this point of the season you're basically hunting in a cooler so get the hide off, the quarters separated, the meat bagged and hung in the shade and you'll be good to go.

Non-Weather Related Factors Affecting Finished Meat Quality

There are a few things other than heat and moisture that may potentially affect the outcome of the quality of your meat. These two things essentially go hand in hand; rigor mortis and adequate aging of the meat. We'll first start with how you can use rigor mortis to your benefit. When an animal first dies it goes through a host of biological changes with the most apparent being rigor mortis. Rigor mortis is the contraction and stiffening of the muscle fibers within the first few hours of death. This process may last anywhere from several hours to a couple days. If you bone-out your quarters immediately upon notching your tag then you may be setting yourself up for an unnecessary increase into the tougher spectrum of meat texture. When a muscle is removed from the bone before rigor mortis has had the chance to fully run its course, then the result will be a muscle that shrinks up into a rock hard wad and does not go back to its original form. When you get this severe contraction of overlapped muscle fibers, then you are increasing the density of these fibers relative to one another. Once you cook this meat, you will see the result of this in the form

(fig. 1) Pictured here are two rear hams from a color phased black bear that I harvested while hunting with my brother in early September one season. The high temps that week were in the 80's and these two quarters, along with the hide and head, hung in this spot overnight and through the first half of the next day and were sufficiently cooled to a manageable temperature once we retrieved them. Notice how they're hanging in game bags and in the shade. There was also a cold flowing creek about 15 yards downslope from here that helped tremendously with them hanging over night and the second load being packed out the following day. This bear was feeding heavily on berries when I shot it and, its diet, paired with utilizing these meat cooling techniques laid the foundation for some amazing tasting bear meat. It went straight into my pre-loaded cooler full of frozen ice jugs as soon as we got back to the trailhead.

of decreased tenderness and an increased chewy consistency. Waiting to de-bone or butcher the quarters until rigor mortis has had enough time to completely go through its process will allow the muscle fibers and connective tissue to relax again, so to speak, which will reduce the muscle fiber overlap leaving you with more tender cuts of meat. It should be noted, however, that waiting to de-bone should only be done if you can sufficiently cool the meat with the bones in wherever you may be. If it's really hot out, say over 70 °F, and you need to quickly cool the back quarter of an elk in September by getting the big bones out, then that always takes precedent over concerns about rigor mortis. Dissipating heat should always be your number one concern. Nothing else matters until you can get that under control. The second non-weather factor affecting your meat happens during the aging process. Assuming you don't have to flash freeze your meat in order to ship it or fly it home from an out-of-state hunt that requires air travel, then it is my opinion that you should always allow time to properly age the meat. If you have to freeze it to fly it home, then it is what it is. The aging process can still occur while in your freezer, albeit minimally compared to pre-frozen aging. When you allow your meat to age, you are essentially promoting the tenderizing of the muscle fibers caused by enzymes breaking down the proteins within the meat. To go about doing this we use an old refrigerator that had the shelves and drawers removed from it and a cross bar installed. Hanging the quarters and scrap bags from this bar for about seven or so days will do wonders to helping you maximize tenderness. If you do not have a spare refrigerator then I recommend you check out Craigslist or OfferUp. You'd be surprised how many used refrigerators are available at a reasonable price on these platforms. This reminds me of a past successful hunt I had… One September day, several years ago, back when Dani and I were in college, I came home with a quartered up mule deer buck that I had killed that morning. Our apartment was only a couple hundred square feet and we barely had enough room in our kitchen for our normal fridge, let alone a spare meat hanging fridge. In my infinite wisdom, I removed the drawers and everything in them from the bottom of the fridge and then placed the quarters in there, stacked up like cord wood. Although thankful for the fresh meat, she was less than thrilled that there were four bloody quarters sharing space with the condiments, the eight different variants of cheese and vegetables that were all nicely organized within the fridge. Even though I would call this a good problem to have, if you can avoid this dilemma with your wife or girlfriend then I would advise you do it at all costs. I probably shouldn't include the fact that I also put the head in a cardboard box in the living room as that was the closest spot to our tiny window mounted air conditioning unit. Anyway, if getting a refrigerator is still not an option, perhaps due to space constraints in your home or garage such as what I experienced, then do the smart thing and look up a local butcher in town who will allow you to hang your meat for a small daily fee. Ideally you will hang the meat where air can circulate around it and in temperatures ranging anywhere from just above freezing to no more than 39 °F.

Field Dressing Techniques

My field dressing process is pretty simple and I will go over it using a September deer hunt as an example. This same process can be used at any time of the year on any big game animal as you can never be too careful when it comes to meat care. As previously mentioned, you need to get the hide off as soon as you can. The higher the ambient temperature is outside, the faster you need to do this. For me, the field dressing technique that I like to use for big game is what is commonly referred to as "the gutless method". This method is just that, gutless. It involves no gutting of the animal and allows you to get all of the meat off without having to handle any of the internal organs, including the entire digestive and urinary tract. If you don't know how to quarter an animal or use the gutless method there are several videos on YouTube that offer great visuals that will get you dialed in. I recommend searching "the gutless method" and finding a video from a reputable source and watching that video several times. Memorizing this technique will help immensely, especially when you've just gotten a big buck down and you're a couple miles from your truck with 5 minutes of daylight left and your adrenaline is redlined. It's not difficult to get a little overwhelmed in this situation but having the knowledge and confidence in your ability to field dress will help you get your buck, and more importantly yourself, back to the truck safely and efficiently. With that being said, here's how I quarter a deer. First, you want to try to find as flat of a spot as possible. When quartering with the gutless method you will want to do one side at a time. Lay the animal on its side and make one long zipper type cut along its back starting at the base of the skull and running along the spine to the top of the tail. Start skinning the hide down toward the belly until you hit the upper portion of the legs. Run another zipper cut along the outside of the front leg and peel the hide away from the meat from the elbow joint up toward the back. Sever the foreleg from the shank and discard. Once you have the hide removed from the front quarter, pull the quarter upward toward the spine and run your blade along the armpit and tight against the rib cage to minimize meat loss. Cut between the rib cage and the shoulder blade until the front quarter is free from the body and place it into a game bag. Find a shaded spot where you can either hang the quarter or lay it on top of some brush or a log until finished. As previously mentioned, the key here is to maximize air circulation around all portions of the meat while keeping the quarter shaded from the sun. Once you have the front quarter removed it is time to repeat on the rear quarter. The rear quarter is pretty similar to the front with one notable exception; there is a ball and socket joint that connects the rear quarter to the animal as opposed to the shoulder blade on the front quarter. Once the hide is removed from the back ham, you will cut at the base of the leg on the inside (toward the center of the spine) of the hip joint until you find the ball and socket. Cut around on the inside (toward the spine) of the ball joint and this will allow the ball, which is the end of the femur bone within the rear quarter, to free itself from the rest of the body. Once you complete this, bag and hang just like the front shoulder. Take extra precautions to not cut too deep while working around the ball joint so you don't accidentally knick the bladder. If this happens, pour clean, cool water on the affected area as soon as possible and then pat dry with a clean cloth if available. This is a fairly common occurrence, so don't freak out. It's not the end of the world and your animal isn't ruined. Just clean it off, dry it out and get back to work. After removing the first two quarters, I then move to the neck meat. Removal of the neck meat doesn't need to be meticulous nor pretty. Just make long slices from below the jaw bone to the upper shoulder. You can remove all of the neck meat from this first side intact if you're planning on making a neck roast or you can hack away and cut it off in several chunks if you're looking to make ground out of it. Just do your best to get as much of the neck meat off as possible. When removing the coveted backstraps, start at whichever end you want. Run your blade at an angle toward and along the spine so you're maximizing the amount of loin that you will be getting. Continue carving along the spine until the backstrap comes free (fig. 2). Undoubtedly the one part of this method that I have seen the most hunters struggle with or be intimidated by is the removal of the tenderloins. This is for good reason too because this is where things can get tricky. In order to remove this cut of meat you will want to locate the last rib back on the animal. Using your free hand, reach underneath the bottom side of the spine and push the gut sack away from you while simultaneously running your knife blade along the underside of the spine, gently pulling the tenderloin away as you carefully cut. The tenderloin will attach several inches up past the last rib so make sure to feel where it connects before you start cutting. This cut of meat is so delicate that you can actual pull the meat off the bone, with minimal force, using your knife blade as a little bit of encouragement along the way. I have found, though, that using your knife will always result in a cleaner cut and removal. Once the tenderloin is removed you should start on the rib meat if you are planning on keeping it. On a deer, there isn't much meat between the ribs so the amount of work and time required may not be worth it to some, but I encourage you to salvage as much meat as you possibly can. On an elk, it's definitely worth it. Once you have completed this side, flip the animal over and repeat. You can remove the head by separating the spinal cord between the base of the skull and the first vertebrae. Contrary to popular belief, you do not need a saw for this. A knife works just fine as long as you actually cut between the vertebrae. There is no pretty way of saying this, but using some twisting and pulling of the head will definitely help you in this process.

Dressing Out Wild Turkey and Upland Birds

You can use the same technique for wild turkey as you do for all upland game birds. Once you get that big Tom that you have been working all morning to finally come into your setup, you will want to breast-out the meat and remove the legs. Lay the bird on its back and locate the knobby point on the upper part of its breast bone. Pull a couple of the feathers away until the skin is exposed then run a small incision down the ridge of the breast big enough to get both of your thumbs in. Once you have a thumb on either side of the breast bone between the skin and meat, forcefully pull the skin away and downward toward the wings. This will allow easy access to all of the meat. Start on one side of the knob at the top of the breast bone and carefully filet the breast out with your knife running down the ridge of the bone. Follow the contour of the rib cage, carving the meat away as

(fig. 2) Pictured here is Michael holding up one of the backstraps from a Mule Deer that he harvested and field dressed using the gutless method. Notice the bagged quarters cooling in the shade in the background.

you go. Once you get the first half of the breast off, repeat on the other side. You can use the same thumb skinning technique on the legs as you did on the breast. Remove the skin from the legs then locate where the ball and socket joint is down at the base of the spine. Carve around the ball joint until the leg comes free. Repeat on the other leg and you are now done processing your thunder chicken. As was stated earlier, you can use this same process on all upland birds including pheasant and grouse. I will include, though, that an extremely quick way to process a grouse (pheasant generally are too large with too much fat for this specific technique to really be effective) is to grab the legs of the bird and place the bird hanging between your legs. With the breast facing out away from you, step on both wings where they connect to the body and slowly pull on the legs upward toward you. If done before rigor mortis sets in, you should have, in your hands, both the legs and the breast meat in one piece. The head and guts will be laying on the ground at this point and you do not have to mess with anything further. Once you have harvested a bird, they can start to get pretty funky rather quickly. The sooner you can get the meat processed and into the cooler then the better off you will be.

Butchering and Freezing

You have now let your animal hang in a refrigerator for a week and you are ready to butcher and package the meat up. For this you will need a high quality knife set, a good meat grinder, a scale and either a vacuum sealer or a bunch of plastic wrap and butcher paper. Cold beer and a butchering team consisting of family members and good buddies is also an added bonus if you can pull it off. In our family we really enjoy this step of the process as it allows for some quality time together and serves as a moment of reverence as we reflect on past hunts.

The Wilderness Kitchen Butchering Process

There are a million ways to butcher an animal but this is the process that we have evolved to work best for us. You will want the surfaces that you will be working on to be as clean as possible. Whether that means laying down a bunch of butcher paper (do not use newspaper as the ink will come off onto your meat) or disinfecting and drying counter tops or flip up tables, this is up to you. I'm not a professional butcher so I'm not going to pretend to know the specific name for each and every cut of meat but I will say that I have cut up dozens of different animals and I have found this to be the easiest and most efficient technique of separating the different cuts of meat. We divide our cuts of meat into four categories; roasts, steaks, backstraps/tenderloins and ground. After reviewing the recipes that Dani has presented for you in the book, you can make the decision of how many of each cut you will want for your cooking needs. We generally grind all of the meat off the front shoulders and the neck then bag the ground meat individually in one pound vacuum sealed bags. This is all of your burgers, tacos, spaghetti, etc. The rear quarters we like to carve into individual roasts first. The different roasts are separated by seams of connective tissue that are very apparent once you are looking at them. Once you get all of the roasts separated then you can decide on how many roasts you will want and how many packages of steaks you will want. For us, steaks are the result of slicing up the roasts into one inch thick medallions. I decide how many steaks will go into each package by how many people we intend to feed with them so this is all personal preference and based on individual needs. Usually it's just me and Dani eating at home so I separate them into meals for two people. This is also very helpful if you are planning on having friends over and making them dinner as you can pull out one package for two people, two packages for four, etc. Packaging roasts is a little more of specific measurement since you will want to cook roasts by themselves but a good general rule of thumb that I have found to work is a deer roast the size of a fist, or about 10 ounces, will feed two adults, assuming you will be having sides as well. Multiply accordingly by X number of fists when deciding how many people you plan on feeding at your future dinner parties or trying to judge how much meat your kids will eat. Once all of the roasts and steaks are packaged and vacuum sealed, I finish up with the backstraps and tenderloin's with each tenderloin getting its own package. I slice the backstraps into medallions approximately ¾" to 1" thick and package using the same technique as the other steaks. Some people like to cut an entire backstrap in half and then freeze to reduce the amount of exposed surface area that comes in contact with frozen air but my backstraps never last long enough for this to be a worry of mine. It's worth noting that you should be labeling every single package of meat with a sharpie before freezing it. I like to include what animal it is, the cut of meat and finally the month/year it was harvested. Separating the different packages of meat into cardboard boxes or plastic bags within your freezer is an easy way to inventory your haul. When all of the cuts of meat are separated and stored together, as well as labeled, then it makes it much easier to pull them out of the freezer to thaw when you're in a hurry to leave for work in the morning. All you have to do is flip through the cookbook and find the meal you want that night then go and grab the corresponding package of meat for that recipe. When you've barely gotten through your first cup of coffee in the morning, you'll be glad that you took the extra minute to organize all of the packages.

Closing Thoughts

I hope you have found this information to be both helpful and useful for your next hunt. There are people who are a bit more cavalier in their meat care then I am and I will say *to each their own* in that regard. They will tell you that field dressing isn't a science and that may be true to them but when you add the science into the process then the quality of your meat will vastly improve. How much enjoyment you get from eating your meat will be directly correlated to how much effort and care you put into the entire process beginning in the field and culminating in your freezer. Now that we've gotten through the nitty gritty portion, I hope you enjoy the meat and potatoes of this cookbook as Dani is truly the best wild game cook that I've ever had the pleasure of dining with. If you follow her recipes as they are presented then you will always be looking forward to your next wild game meal.

Sausage

Biscuits and Gravy

Sausage Rolls

Sausage and Egg Scramble

Biscuits and Elk Sausage Gravy

Biscuits and Gravy is the perfect meal for those days when you need a hearty, comforting breakfast, and is also great for entertaining because the recipe serves about 4 people and can easily be doubled. You or your local butcher can make sausage out of most wild game and in a pinch, this recipe works great with pork sausage as well. If your wild game sausage doesn't produce much grease, I suggest adding a tablespoon of butter before mixing in the flour when making your gravy.

serves 4 | prep 10 min | cook 20 min

Ingredients

For the Biscuits
2 cups flour
1 tablespoon baking powder
1 teaspoon salt
1 stick salted butter
1 cup milk

For the Gravy
1 pound elk sausage
2 tablespoons flour
2 cups milk
½ teaspoon salt
½ teaspoon pepper
½ teaspoon garlic powder
½ teaspoon onion powder

Instructions

To make the biscuits: Mix the flour, baking powder and salt together in a large mixing bowl. Cut the butter into small pieces and incorporate into the flour mixture. Slowly add the milk and mix until all ingredients are combined. Add more flour in tablespoon increments if your batter is too wet (you want the batter to hold it's shape). Scoop large spoonful's (about 2 inches in diameter) of the dough onto a baking sheet lined with parchment paper. Cook at 425 ºF until the tops of the biscuits turn golden brown, about 8 minutes.

To make the gravy: In a large pan, begin browning the sausage over medium heat. Once the sausage has almost no pink left, turn the heat down to medium-low and add the two tablespoons of flour to the pan, mixing it in with the sausage grease. If your sausage doesn't produce much grease, you can add 1 tablespoon of butter to the pan and incorporate it with the flour. Once all the flour and sausage grease are combined, slowly whisk in the milk and bring the mixture to a boil. Turn the heat down to low and simmer until the gravy has thickened, about 5 minutes. Serve the gravy over broken up biscuits and enjoy.

Sausage Rolls

Sausage Rolls

Sausage rolls are a traditional English appetizer that my family makes for special events, parties and holidays. It doesn't feel like Christmas until the smell of sausage rolls fills my house. I've adapted my family's sausage roll recipe using wild game sausage instead of pork sausage, but either will work. Also, if you don't feel like making your own puff pastry, there are some great pre-made ones you can buy at most grocery stores. I use these when I don't have time to make my own.

serves 10-12 | prep 1 hour | cook 40 min

Ingredients

For the Pastry
2 cups flour, sifted
1 teaspoon salt
6 ounces cold lard
6 ounces cold butter
1 teaspoon lemon juice
½ cup water

For the Meat
1 pound wild game sausage
2 eggs
½ cup breadcrumbs

Note:

When working with puff pastry, make sure not to handle it too much. You want to ensure the butter stays in clumps and doesn't melt into the pastry. If your pastry is getting to warm, stick in the freezer instead of the fridge for a few minutes.

Instructions

To make the pastry: Combine the flour and salt in a large mixing bowl. Cut the butter and lard into 1 inch cubes. Add the butter and lard cubes to the flour, then pour in the lemon juice and half of the water. Stir to combine the water and flour, leaving the butter and lard in clumps. Squish the mixture into a 4" x 4" square, wrap in wax paper and refrigerate for at least 15 minutes. Unwrap the mixture, place it on a heavily floured surface and roll it into a 4" x 10" rectangle. Fold the pastry mixture into thirds, then rewrap and refrigerate another 15 minutes. Repeat the process of rolling out the pastry, folding and refrigerating three times. The goal is to disperse the lard and butter throughout the pastry without allowing it to melt.

To make the meat mixture: In a mixing bowl, add the sausage, 1 egg, and the breadcrumbs. Combine thoroughly.

To assemble: Preheat your oven to 400 °F. Roll out the pastry into a 18" x 12" rectangle, then separate into three 18" x 4" strips. Take a third of the sausage, roll into a 1" thick log and place it along the middle of one of the pastry strips. Fold the pastry over the sausage, and seal with a little water. Repeat this step with the rest of the sausage and the remaining two pastry strips. Cut each roll into individual 1" pieces, then brush with a beaten egg. Cut two small slits into the top of each roll to let out any steam while baking. Bake at 350 °F until the pastry turns golden brown. Serve hot.

Elk Sausage and Egg Scramble

serves 4 | prep 10 min | cook 20 min

Ingredients

1 pound elk sausage
1 tablespoon olive oil
1 bell pepper, chopped
½ an onion, chopped
1 cup fresh spinach
¼ cup sliced mushrooms
(optional)
6 eggs, beaten
2 ounces cheddar cheese,
grated
1 teaspoon salt
1 teaspoon pepper

Instructions

In a large pan, heat the olive oil over medium-high heat. Add the onions and bell pepper and sauté until they are soft. Add in the sausage and begin to brown until there is no pink left. Drain any excess oil, then add the spinach and mushrooms. Turn the heat down to medium. Once the spinach has wilted, add the eggs and stir regularly until cooked through. Serve either as a scramble or wrap in a flour tortilla, add some salsa and serve as a breakfast burrito.

Ground

Venison Bolognese

Venison Street Tacos

Meatballs and Mashed Potatoes

Bacon Blue Burger

Wild Game Lasagna

Elk Chili

Venison Pasty

Wild Game Pizza

Shepherd's Pie

Elwell Meatloaf

Venison Bolognese

This recipe should really be called Venison Bolognese-ish. I add a variety of herbs that are not traditionally included in Bolognese sauce and I don't add milk. I guess you wouldn't even really call it a Bolognese, but that's the closest thing to what this sauce is. I really love this dish because it is more exciting than regular spaghetti and the combination of the herbs, broth and wine give this sauce a deep flavor and a lovely aroma. This sauce can also be used in the lasagna recipe found on page 33.

Venison Bolognese

serves 4 | prep 10 min | cook 2 hour 20 min

Ingredients

4 slices bacon, chopped
¼ an onion, chopped
2 cloves garlic, minced
2 celery stalks, chopped
1 medium carrot, chopped
1 pound ground venison
¼ cup beef broth
¼ cup red wine
1 (14 ounce) can tomato sauce
1 (14 ounce) can petite diced tomatoes
5-6 fresh basil leaves, torn (*or 2 teaspoons dried basil*)
1 teaspoon dried oregano
1 teaspoon dried rosemary
2 bay leaves
Dash of cinnamon
½ cup finely grated parmesan (more for garnish)
1 package fettuccini noodles

Instructions

In a large pot, begin cooking the bacon over medium heat until they are almost crispy. Drain most of the grease, leaving approximately ½ of a tablespoon to cook the vegetables in. Add the chopped onion, garlic, celery and carrots and sauté until the onions begin to turn translucent. Add in the ground venison and cook until it is almost completely brown. Pour in the beef broth and wine, turn the temperature down to medium-low and simmer for about 5 minutes. Add in the tomato sauce and diced tomatoes, basil, oregano, rosemary, bay leaves and cinnamon. Let the sauce simmer for 2 hours. You could also transfer the sauce to a crock pot at this stage and cook on low for a few hours if you wanted to let the sauce cook unattended. When the sauce has about 30 minutes left, add in the parmesan cheese and cook the final 30 minutes.

Once the sauce is nearly done, set a pot of water to boil. Cook the fettuccini noodles to al dente, according to the package instructions. When the noodles are done, remove them from the water, making sure to save about ¼ cup of the cooking water. Return the noodles to the pot, pour the saved cooking water over them, then add the sauce. Dish the pasta onto a plate and serve immediately, topped with freshly grated parmesan and a basil leaf if desired.

Venison Street Tacos

Venison Street Tacos

Tacos are probably one of the easiest ways to cook any ground wild game. They make an almost weekly appearance in our house and are just one of those things that everyone loves. You can make this recipe with any ground meat you have, whether it's wild game, or store bought ground beef or turkey. It'll all taste great! Sometimes, instead of water, I will add in ½ a beer to give the tacos a little added flavor.

Serves 4 | prep 10 min | cook 10 min

Ingredients

1 tablespoon olive oil
1 pound ground venison
1 tablespoon chili powder
½ tablespoon cumin
1 clove garlic, minced
½ an onion, finely chopped
½ teaspoon paprika
½ teaspoon salt
½ teaspoon pepper
Dash of cayenne pepper to taste
½ cup water (*or beer*)
Tortillas or taco shells
Choice of toppings

Instructions

In a large frying pan, heat the olive oil over medium-high heat. Add the garlic and onion and sauté for a minute or two until soft, making sure not to burn the garlic. Next, add the ground meat and cook until brown, about 5 minutes. Drain any liquid from the pan if you have it, though there may be none because wild game is so lean. Add the seasonings and ½ a cup of water (or beer). Reduce the heat to low and simmer until the water is evaporated, about five minutes. Remove from heat and serve immediately. I like to serve these on small corn tortillas with some lettuce, homemade guacamole, diced tomatoes, queso fresco, and some fresh cilantro.

Wilderness Kitchen Guacamole

In a large mixing bowl, add 1 diced avocado, 1 tablespoon of finely chopped cilantro, ½ teaspoon of each garlic powder, onion powder, and salt. Add in a dash of pepper, 1 teaspoon of fresh lime juice, 1 teaspoon of Worcestershire sauce, and a healthy dash of your favorite hot sauce. Mash all the ingredients together and add more of any to taste.

Meatballs and Mashed Potatoes

Meatballs and Mashed Potatoes

serves 4 | prep 20 min | cook 45 min

Ingredients

For the Meatballs
1 pound ground game meat
¼ cup breadcrumbs
½ an onion, finely chopped
1 tablespoon parsley, finely chopped (more for garnish)
1 egg
1 teaspoon salt
1 teaspoon pepper
½ teaspoon garlic powder
3 tablespoons olive oil
1 cup of flour

For the Mashed Potatoes
3 large russet potatoes
¼ cup heavy whipping cream
2 tablespoons butter
2 tablespoons sour cream
½ teaspoon salt
¼ teaspoon pepper
¼ teaspoon garlic powder
¼ teaspoon onion powder

For the Gravy
2 tablespoons butter
2 tablespoons flour
2 cups beef broth

Instructions

To make the meatballs: In a large mixing bowl, combine all the meatball ingredients except the olive oil and flour. Take a large spoonful of the meat mixture and roll into a ball about 2" in diameter, making sure to pack the meatball as tightly as possible, and set aside. Repeat with the remaining meat mixture. Once all the meatballs are formed, heat the olive oil in a large frying pan over medium-high heat. Place the flour on a plate and roll each meatball in the flour, making sure to coat them thoroughly. When the oil reaches temperature, add the meatballs to the frying pan. As the meatballs begin cooking on the outside, rotate them regularly so the entire outside gets crispy. Cook until the internal temperature of the meatballs reach 135 °F.

To make the potatoes: Bring a large pot of salted water to a boil (you want to make sure you have enough water to cover the potatoes). Peel the potatoes and cut them into equal pieces around 1-2" in size. When the water begins boiling, place the potatoes into the pot and boil until a fork can easily pierce through them. Remove the potatoes, drain the water, and return the potatoes to the pot. Add the butter, cream, sour cream and spices and begin mashing the potatoes with a potato masher or electric mixer. Mash to your desired level of smoothness.

To make the gravy: In a saucepan, melt the butter over medium-low heat. Add the flour and mix completely. Slowly whisk in the beef broth, making sure to smooth out any clumps that may form. Turn the gravy down to a simmer and allow to thicken, usually 2-3 minutes.

To assemble: Place a generous scoop of mashed potatoes on a plate, then place 3-4 meatballs on top of the potatoes. Pour gravy over the top and sprinkle with some fresh parsley if desired.

Bacon Blue Burger

Who doesn't love burger night? I seriously wish every night could be burger night and this burger recipe is my absolute favorite. If you aren't blue cheese obsessed like I am, you can easily substitute it with your favorite cheese and still love this burger as much as I do. One important thing to remember when cooking wild game burgers is to make sure you sear the first side of the burger enough so it doesn't fall apart. This is especially important if you are going to cook your burgers on the barbecue.

serves 4 | prep 15 min | cook 10 min

Ingredients

1 pound ground elk
½ cup breadcrumbs
1 egg
1 tablespoon olive oil
½ cup blue cheese crumbles
(*or other cheese preference*)
4 slices bacon
Choice of bun and toppings

Instructions

Place the ground elk, breadcrumbs and egg in a bowl and mix until combined. Adding the egg and breadcrumbs will help bind the burgers together. Divide the mixture into four equal portions. To form the patties, roll each ¼ pound portion into a ball, then squish firmly into the shape of a burger patty. In a frying pan, heat the olive oil over medium-high heat. When the oil is hot, gently place each burger patty into the pan. You want to make sure to get a really good sear on the first side which will ensure that your burgers don't fall apart (but make sure not to burn it). Once the first side is cooked, flip the burgers and cook to your preference, though I suggest cooking to medium rare. Remove the burgers from the pan, top with some blue cheese crumbles, and let rest while the cheese melts a little.

I like to serve these burgers with lettuce, tomato, pickles, mayonnaise, mustard and a nice heaping pile of French fries on the side.

Wild Game Lasagna

Wild Game Lasagna

serves 10 | prep 30 min | cook 1 hour 15 min

Ingredients

For the Sauce

1 pound ground game meat
2 tablespoons olive oil
2 cloves garlic, minced
1 onion
2 (14 ounce) cans petite diced tomatoes
1 (14 ounce) can tomato sauce
1 (6 ounce) can tomato paste
5-6 fresh basil leaves, torn (*or 2 teaspoons dried basil*)
1 teaspoon dried oregano
1 teaspoon dried rosemary
1 teaspoon dried thyme
½ teaspoon nutmeg
2 teaspoons salt
1 teaspoon pepper

For the Lasagna

1 package lasagna noodles (cooked according to package instructions)
8 ounces ricotta cheese
½ pound mozzarella cheese (shredded or sliced)
1 cup parmesan cheese

Instructions

To make the sauce: In a large sauce pan, heat the olive oil over medium heat. Add the garlic and onion and gently sauté until the onions become translucent, making sure not to burn the garlic. Add in the ground meat and cook until brown. Drain any excess grease, then stir in the tomatoes, tomato sauce, tomato paste, and spices. Simmer anywhere from 30 minutes to a couple hours, until you are ready to assemble your lasagna.

To assemble: Take about 1 cup (or more if needed) of your sauce and cover the bottom of a 15" by 10" baking dish. Place a layer of noodles down on top of the sauce. Add another layer of meat sauce on top of the noodles, then a layer of ricotta cheese. If you are using sliced mozzarella, evenly place the slices on top of the ricotta cheese, or if you are using grated, sprinkle a layer of grated mozzarella over the ricotta. Sprinkle some parmesan cheese, then add another layer of meat sauce. Repeat this process with the remaining ingredients. I usually make the last layer a layer of noodles, a thin layer of meat sauce, and a layer of mozzarella and parmesan, depending on what I have left. Bake at 375 °F for about 45 minutes.

Elk Chili

Elk Chili

Ingredients

1 pound ground elk
1 tablespoon olive oil
½ an onion, diced
1 (14 ounce) can red kidney beans, drained and rinsed
2 (14 ounce) cans chili beans (with liquid)
2 tablespoons chili powder
1 teaspoon garlic powder
Dash of cayenne pepper to taste

Instructions

In a pan, heat the olive oil over medium-high heat. Add the onions and sauté until they are soft. Add the ground elk and cook until brown. Drain the grease from the meat, then place the mixture into a crock pot. Add the rinsed kidney beans, the chili beans (with liquid), and the spices. Turn your crock pot on low and cook for 8 hours.

If you don't have a crockpot, this can also be cooked in a large stock pot on the stove over low heat and simmer until the beans are soft, usually 1-2 hours. If using this method, make sure to watch the chili and stir it frequently, ensuring the beans don't stick to the bottom and burn.

Serve with bread or saltine crackers, or over a bed of rice if you prefer.

Venison Pasty

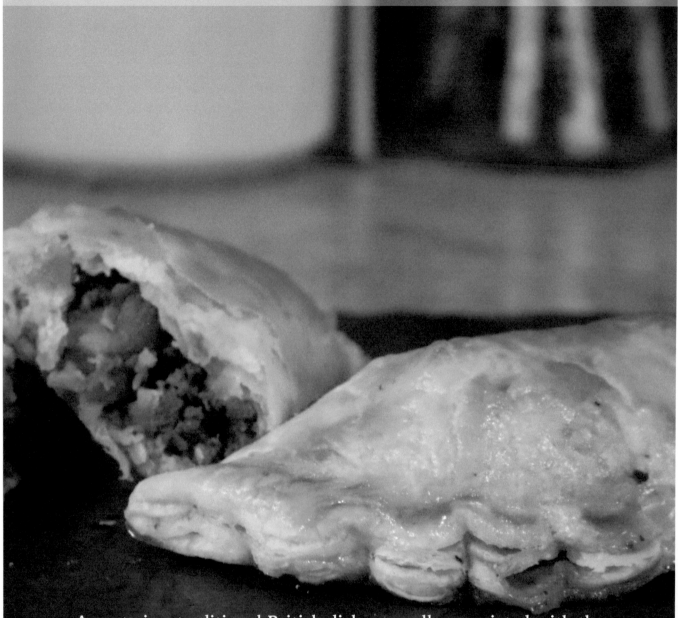

A pasty is a traditional British dish generally associated with the county of Cornwall. They were a meal often eaten by coal miners due to the fact that they are a full meal contained in pastry, they are durable, and can be eaten without utensils. My family has been making them for generations and now, I make them with venison or elk. They are great for camping, hunting, or even just to freeze and take out for a quick and easy lunch when needed. This recipe works great with ground beef as well.

Venison Pasty

serves 6-8 | prep 1 hour | cook 1 hour

Ingredients

For the Pastry
3 cups flour
1 teaspoon salt
1½ cups cold butter
¼ cup ice water

For the Meat Filling
1 tablespoon olive oil
1 onion, chopped
2 cloves garlic, finely chopped
1 cup carrots, chopped
1 pound ground venison
1 large boiled potato, cut into
¼ inch cubes
1 tablespoon flour
½ cup red wine
1½ cup beef broth
1 egg, beaten

Instructions

To make the pastry: In a food processer, add two cups of the flour, leaving one cup for flouring your rolling surface. Cut the butter into ¼ inch cubes, making sure to keep it cold, then add it to the food processor. Pulse the food processor while slowly adding in the ice water, little by little. Pulse until the butter and flour are somewhat combined, looking like large breadcrumbs. Remove the mixture from the food processor, shape into a 2" by 4" rectangle, then wrap in saran wrap and place in the refrigerator for 15 minutes. Remove the pastry from the refrigerator and unwrap. Place the pastry on a floured surface and roll it into a 4" by 10" rectangle. Fold the pastry into thirds, then rewrap and refrigerate another 15 minutes. Repeat the process of rolling out the pastry, folding and refrigerating, three more times. Roll the pastry out in a large sheet until it is less than a ¼" thick. Using an upturned bowl as a stencil, cut out circles in the pastry, about 6-8" in diameter.

To make the meat filling: In a large stock pot, begin heating the olive oil over medium heat. When the oil reaches temperature, add in the onions, garlic and carrots, and begin sautéing until the onions are translucent. Add in the ground venison and cook until it turns brown. Add in the flour and combine with the grease, then add in the wine and broth, mixing well. Finally, add the potatoes and cook on low for 30 minutes. Remove the mixture from the heat when the potatoes are easily pierced with a fork, but don't break. Allow the mixture to cool completely.

To assemble: Spoon about ¾ cup of the mixture onto the middle of one of the pastry circles. Wet the edge of the pastry, then fold the circle in half, encasing the meat mixture. Press the edges together, then crimp to ensure it stays. Repeat with the remaining meat mixture and pastry circles. Brush the pasties with the beaten egg and bake at 425 °F for 20-30 minutes, or until the pasties are golden brown on top.

Wild Game Pizza

Wild Game Pizza

This wild game pizza is a great way to combine many different types of game meat. You can use any game meat you have in the freezer really, and can even substitute the venison for ground beef and the elk sausage for pork sausage if needed. You can also use regular pepperoni instead of summer sausage, though the summer sausage adds a really nice smoky flavor to this pizza. You can include any other toppings you would like such as mushrooms or black olives. This dough recipe makes enough for two medium pizzas.

serves 8 | prep 20 min | cook 20 min

Ingredients

For the Pizza Dough
1 packet instant dry yeast
1½ teaspoon sugar
2 cups flour (more for rolling surface)
1 teaspoon salt
¾ cup warm water
3 tablespoons olive oil

For the Toppings
1 (14 ounce) jar pizza sauce
3 cups shredded mozzarella cheese
¼ pound ground venison
¼ pound elk sausage
¼ pound bear summer sausage (or pepperoni)
Any other choice of toppings (such as olives, mushrooms, peppers, etc.)

Instructions

To make the dough: Preheat your oven to 425 °F. In a large mixing bowl, combine the yeast, sugar, salt, and half of the flour. Mix in the water and oil, then slowly mix in the rest of the flour. If your dough is too sticky to work with, add in more flour until you get a nice elastic feel to it. Remove the dough from the bowl and begin to knead it for about 5 minutes, adding more flour if necessary. Split the dough in half and form each half into a ball. Roll each ball into a large circle, about 1 foot in diameter. If you are only going to make one pizza, freeze one of the balls of dough instead of rolling it out.

To assemble: Brown the ground venison and the elk sausage separately and set aside. Slice the summer sausage into thin slices. Spread the pizza sauce over the dough, leaving about ¼" of space around the edge for the crust. Sprinkle about 2 cups of the mozzarella cheese over the sauce, then spread your desired amount of each meat over the pizza. Add any other toppings you wish, then sprinkle with the rest of the mozzarella as desired. On a baking sheet or pizza stone, cook on center rack for about 20 minutes, or until the crust turns brown and the cheese begins to bubble.

Shepherd's Pie

Shepherd's Pie

serves 6 | prep 10 min | cook 50 min

Ingredients	Instructions

For the Meat Filling

2 tablespoons olive oil
2 cloves garlic, minced
½ cup onion, chopped
½ cup celery, chopped
½ cup frozen peas
½ cup carrots, chopped
1 pound ground venison
2 tablespoons flour
1 cup beef broth
1 tablespoon Worcestershire sauce
1 tablespoon red wine
½ teaspoon salt
½ teaspoon rosemary
½ teaspoon thyme
¼ teaspoon pepper

For the Potatoes

3 large russet potatoes
¼ cup heavy whipping cream
2 tablespoons butter
2 tablespoons sour cream
½ teaspoon salt
¼ teaspoon pepper
¼ teaspoon garlic powder
¼ teaspoon onion powder

To make the meat filling: Preheat your oven to 400 °F. In a large pan, heat the olive oil over medium heat. Add the garlic, onion, celery, peas and carrots to the pan and sauté gently, making sure not to burn the garlic. Once the vegetables are soft, add in the ground meat and begin to brown. Once the meat has browned, add in the flour and incorporate into the grease from the meat. Whisk in the beef broth, Worcestershire sauce and red wine, combining thoroughly with the flour. Turn the temperature down to medium-low and bring to a simmer. Add in the salt, rosemary, thyme and pepper and allow the sauce to thicken, about 5 minutes.

Once the sauce in the meat mixture has thickened to a gravy, remove it from the heat and let it cool. Once cool, spread the mixture into a pie dish and smooth to an even surface, pressing down softly to make a somewhat firm surface for the potatoes.

To make the potatoes: Bring a large pot of salted water to a boil (you want to make sure you have enough water to cover the potatoes). Peel the potatoes and cut them into equal pieces around 1-2" in size. When the water begins to boil, place the potatoes in the pot and boil until a fork can easily pierce through them. Remove the potatoes, drain the water, and return the potatoes to the pot. Add the butter, cream, sour cream and spices and begin mashing the potatoes with a potato masher or electric mixer. Mash to your desired level of smoothness.

To Assemble: Gently spoon the mashed potatoes over the meat mix and carefully spread them out until smooth, making sure not to pick the meat mixture up into the potatoes. Bake for about 30 minutes or until the potatoes begin to turn golden brown. Serve either on it's own or topped with gravy.

Elwell Meatloaf

This meatloaf recipe is adapted from Michael's mother, Maureen Elwell. It is by far the best meatloaf I have ever had. If you don't have wild game, you can substitute the wild game sausage with pork sausage and the ground venison or elk with ground beef.

serves 8 | prep 10 min | cook 1 hour

Ingredients

1 pound wild game sausage
1 pound ground venison or elk
¼ onion, finely chopped
1 clove garlic, minced
¼ cup breadcrumbs
1 egg

Instructions

Preheat your oven to 350 °F. In a mixing bowl, combine all the ingredients and mix well. Place the mixture in a bread or meatloaf pan and squish into all the sides, making sure the top is even. Place the meatloaf in the oven and cook for 1 hour or until it reaches an internal temperature of about 165 °F. Serve with mashed potatoes and brown gravy (see meatball recipe on page 28).

Steaks

Wild Steak Oscar

Sizzling Venison Fajitas

Backstrap and Bacon Blue Salad

Marinated Tenderloin and Grilled Summer Vegetables

Backstrap and Mediterranean Salad with Balsamic Drizzle

Tenderloin Jalapeño Poppers

Wild Cheesesteak Sandwich

Wild Steak Oscar

Wild Steak Oscar

In our house, we don't eat out very much. Instead, we just make fancy dinners at home for half the price. This recipe is our go to date night dish. It's relatively easy and so delicious. The hollandaise sauce can make this recipe a little tricky, but if you aren't comfortable making your own hollandaise, you can buy a hollandaise mix from the grocery store. It makes this meal much easier and is something I do when I'm not up to making it fresh. As a bonus, if you have any leftover crab meat, use it in our crab cakes recipe on page 86.

serves 2 | prep 30 min | cook 10 min

Ingredients

For the Steak
Backstrap medallions (1-2 per person)
1 tablespoon grass fed butter
1 Dungeness crab, cleaned and deshelled

For the Hollandaise
2 egg yolks
1 tablespoon fresh lemon juice
Dash of salt
Cayenne pepper to taste
1 stick melted butter

Instructions

To cook the backstrap medallions: In a frying pan, melt the grass fed butter over high heat. Once melted, add the backstrap medallions, then immediately turn the pan down to medium-high heat, ensuring you get a good initial sear. Cook the medallions for about 2-3 minutes per side, or until the internal temperature reaches 125 °F. Remove the medallions from the heat and let sit for about 5 minutes. While the steaks are resting, make your hollandaise sauce.

To make the hollandaise: In a stainless steel bowl, whisk together the lemon juice and egg yolks. Whisk until the mixture is bubbly and has increased in volume. Place the mixing bowl over a pan full of water that is set at a gentle simmer. Once the mixture has thickened slightly, slowly add in the butter, whisking constantly. Continue to whisk until the sauce is thick and creamy, then add in the salt and cayenne pepper. Use immediately.

To assemble: Place each medallion on a plate and top with a spoonful of crab meat. Pour the hollandaise over the crab and serve immediately. I like to serve this meal with a side of oven roasted asparagus and some lemon-parmesan orzo pasta.

Sizzling Venison Fajitas

Sizzling Venison Fajitas

serves 4 | prep 20 min | cook 10 min

Ingredients

1 pound venison steaks
½ tablespoon chili powder
1 tablespoon cumin
½ teaspoon paprika
½ teaspoon salt
½ teaspoon pepper
Cayenne Pepper to taste
1 tablespoon lime juice
1 tablespoon Worcestershire sauce
2 tablespoons olive oil divided
1 green bell pepper
1 red bell pepper
1 clove garlic, finely chopped
½ an onion

Instructions

Cut the steaks into ¼" thick strips. To make the seasoning mixture combine the chili powder, cumin, paprika, salt, pepper and cayenne pepper in a small bowl. In a resealable bag, combine the lime juice, Worcestershire sauce, and 1 tablespoon of the olive oil. Add in the steak and half of the seasoning mixture, mix together, and set in the fridge for at least 1 hour. Cut the bell peppers and onions into strips about ¼" thick. In a large frying pan, heat the remaining olive oil over medium-high heat. Add the onion and garlic and cook for a minute or two, then add the bell peppers. Cook the vegetables until they begin to soften. Add in the steak and the remaining seasoning mixture, mixing both in with the cooking vegetables. Cook the fajita mixture until the steak is cooked to your liking. I recommend cooking the venison steak to medium rare, but if you want your meat a little more well done, that's ok with this recipe. Remove the steak and veggies from heat and serve immediately. I serve my fajitas with flour tortillas, lettuce, Wilderness Kitchen guacamole (see page 27), sour cream and cheddar cheese.

Backstrap and Bacon Blue Salad

Backstrap and Bacon Blue Salad

serves 2 | prep 10 min | cook 10 min

Ingredients

4 backstrap medallions
½ teaspoon garlic powder
½ teaspoon onion powder
1 tablespoon grass fed butter
½ teaspoon salt
½ teaspoon pepper
4 cups baby spring mix lettuce
Blue cheese dressing
4 slices of bacon
¼ red onion, thinly sliced
½ cup croutons

Instructions

For the backstrap: In a frying pan, heat the butter over high heat for a minute or two. Once the butter is hot, add the backstrap medallions to the pan. You want to make sure you hear a nice sizzle when you add the steaks to the pan, ensuring you get a good sear. Turn the pan down to medium-high heat and evenly sprinkle with the garlic and onion powder. Cook the backstraps for 2-3 minutes per side. Check the temperature of your steaks and remove when they reach 125 °F. Sprinkle the steaks with salt and pepper and let rest for at least five minutes.

For the salad: Cut your bacon into small pieces and cook in a frying pan over medium-high heat until crispy. Remove from the heat and set aside. Place the lettuce in a salad bowl and add the the blue cheese dressing, tossing the lettuce to coat completely. Add in the bacon, croutons, onion and any other salad toppings you would like to add.

To serve: You can either cut the backstrap medallions into ½" in strips and serve over the top of your salad or you can keep them whole and serve the salad on the side.

Marinated Tenderloin and Grilled Summer Vegetables

Marinated Tenderloin and Grilled Summer Vegetables

serves 2-4 | prep 4 hours and 20 min | cook 10 min

Ingredients

For the Marinade
1 venison or elk tenderloin
2 tablespoons Worcestershire sauce
2 tablespoons soy sauce
¼ teaspoon salt
¼ teaspoon pepper

For the Vegetables
1 medium yellow zucchini
1 orange bell pepper
1 red onion
6 cremini mushrooms
8-10 asparagus stalks
2 tablespoons olive oil
1 teaspoon sea salt

Note:

Feel free to add any summer vegetables you find or anything you might have growing in your garden. Have fun with it!

Instructions

Place the tenderloin in a glass dish and, using a fork, poke several small holes throughout the meat. Cover the tenderloin with the Worcestershire sauce and soy sauce and then sprinkle with salt and pepper. Cover the dish with saran wrap and place in the refrigerator for at least 4 hours, flipping it over half way through.

Once the tenderloin has marinated for a few hours, remove it from the refrigerator and bring it to room temperature.

Preheat your barbecue on high for 10 minutes. While the barbecue is heating, cut all the vegetables into bite sized chunks. Place the vegetables in a bowl and coat in olive oil and sea salt. Take the vegetable pieces and place them on barbecue skewers.

Once the barbecue is hot, place the tenderloin on one side and the vegetable skewers on the other side. Turn the barbecue down to medium heat. Cook for about 3 minutes then flip both the tenderloin and the vegetables skewers over and cook the other side for about another 3 minutes. Check the internal temperature of the meat and remove from the barbecue once the temperature reaches 125 °F. Remove the vegetables when they become cooked to your preference (make sure to remove if they begin to blacken).

Cut the tenderloin into ¾" slices and serve with the vegetables on or off the skewers.

Backstrap and Mediterranean Salad with Balsamic Drizzle

Backstrap and Mediterranean Salad with Balsamic Drizzle

This salad is a perfect dish for the summer or for when you are looking for something easy and healthy. The best part about this dish is that it's so versatile. You can easily swap out the balsamic dressing with your favorite one, the vegetables for whatever you have in your fridge, or even the meat with what is in the freezer. Backstrap from any large game animal will work.

serves 2 | prep 10 min | cook 10 min

Ingredients

4 backstrap medallions
1 tablespoon grass fed butter
½ teaspoon salt
½ teaspoon pepper
½ cup balsamic vinegar
4 cups baby spring mix lettuce
¼ cup Kalamata olives, sliced in half
¼ cup feta cheese sprinkles
¼ cup cucumber, diced
¼ cup artichoke hearts, diced
½ a red onion, thinly sliced
1 cup balsamic dressing

Instructions

For the backstrap: In a frying pan, heat the butter over high heat for a minute or two. Once the butter is hot, add the backstrap medallions to the pan. You want to make sure you hear a nice sizzle when you add the steaks to the pan, ensuring you get a good sear. Turn the pan down to medium-high heat and evenly sprinkle with the garlic and onion powder. Cook the backstraps for 2-3 minutes per side. Check the temperature of your steaks and remove when they reach 125 °F. Sprinkle the steaks with salt and pepper and let rest for at least five minutes.

For the balsamic drizzle: In a sauce pan, heat the balsamic vinegar over medium-high heat. Once the vinegar begins to boil, turn the heat down to low and simmer for about 5-10 minutes, stirring occasionally. The vinegar will begin to reduce and become thicker. You will know it's done when the reduction begins to stick to your spoon. Make sure not to cook it too fast or you will create balsamic candy.

For the salad: In a large bowl, toss the lettuce with the balsamic dressing. Place about 2 cups of the lettuce on a plate. Sprinkle half of the olives, feta cheese, cucumber, artichoke hearts, and onions over the lettuce. Place the slices of backstrap over the salad, then drizzle the balsamic reduction over the top.

Tenderloin Jalapeño Poppers

Tenderloin Jalapeño Poppers

serves 12 | prep 20 min | cook 10 min

Ingredients

1 pound elk tenderloin
12 jalapenos
1 (8 ounce) package sour cream
1 (12 ounce) package bacon

Instructions

Cut your tenderloin into bite size pieces. Halve the jalapeños lengthwise and hollow out the seeds. Cut the bacon slices in half. Transfer the cream cheese into a pastry tube or a plastic bag with the corner cut (if the cream cheese is too cold to squeeze from the bag, microwave for about ten seconds to soften.) Fill each jalapeño half with cream cheese, then place a piece of tenderloin on the cream cheese. Wrap the entire thing with half a slice of bacon and put a toothpick through the side to keep the bacon in place. Barbecue the poppers on medium-low heat until the bacon is fully cooked.

Wild Cheesesteak Sandwich

serves 2 | prep 10 min | cook 10 min

Ingredients

½ pound elk or deer steak
1 green bell pepper
1 yellow onion
2 tablespoon olive oil
¼ teaspoon salt
¼ teaspoon pepper
4 slices provolone cheese
2 hoagie rolls

Instructions

Cut the steak, bell pepper and onion into thin strips, about ¼" thick. In a large frying pan, heat the olive oil over medium-high heat. Add the bell pepper and onions and sauté until the onions are translucent and the peppers begin to soften. While the vegetables are cooking, sprinkle the steak with salt and pepper. Add the steak to the frying pan and cook to desired level of doneness. Remove the veggie and steak mixture and place on a hoagie roll, then cover with the provolone cheese. Put the sandwiches in the oven set to broil and allow the cheese to melt, about two minutes. Serve immediately.

Roasts

Venison Roasts and Yorkshire Pudding

Venison Pot Roast

Venison Wellington

Venison Roast and Yorkshire Puddings

Venison Roast and Yorkshire Puddings

In my family, there was nothing better than a long weekend of skiing followed by our family's traditional Sunday meal of roast beef and Yorkshire pudding. We would come home on Sunday, still in our long johns, and the whole family would get to cooking; my specialty was always the gravy. It was a tradition I knew I would carry on to my own household one day.

Serves 6 | prep 20 min | cook 1 hour

Ingredients

For the Roast
1 (3 pound) deer or elk roast
Seasoning salt

For the Yorkshire Pudding
1 cup flour
1 cup milk
4 eggs
Vegetable oil

Note

Serve the venison roast and Yorkshire puddings with a side of roasted vegetables and smothered in gravy.

Instructions

To cook the roast: Preheat your oven to 425 °F. Cover the roast in seasoning salt and place on a roast pan. Place the roast in the oven for about 10 minutes. After cooking it in the oven at the high temperature, turn the oven down to 350 °F and cook for another 20 minutes. Check the temperature of the roast after 20 minutes and add more time in 5 minute increments until the meat reaches 125 °F. Remove the roast from the oven, cover with foil and let rest at least ten minutes.

To cook the Yorkshire Puddings: Once the roast is finished, bring the oven temperature back up to 425 °F. In a large mixing bowl, add the flour and make a well by pushing some of the flour to the sides of the bowl. Crack the eggs into the well. With a fork, begin beating the eggs, then start gradually bringing in flour from the sides of the bowl while slowly adding the milk to the mixture. Mix well until the milk, flour and eggs are combined and all the clumps are gone. In a 6 cup muffin pan, add just enough vegetable oil to cover the bottom of each cup. Put the pan with the oil in the oven for 5 minutes. After five minutes, carefully remove the pan and oil and quickly add about a quarter cup of the batter to each cup. You want to work fast and get the pan back into the oven as quickly as possible. Set the timer for 20 minutes and do not open the oven before it goes off. If you let any heat out of the oven, the Yorkshire puddings won't rise properly. After the 20 minutes are up, you can crack the oven quickly to check on the Yorkshire puddings. When the tops are golden brown, remove them from the oven and serve immediately.

Venison Pot Roast

Venison Pot Roast

Pot roast is a favorite of ours for cozy winter days. The best part about this roast is that it is made in the crockpot so it's a perfect meal to start in the morning and come back to after a long day of hunting in cold weather. It's also very easy and straightforward. The most important part is getting a good sear before throwing it in the crockpot to ensure it keeps a lot of the moisture inside. This can serve around 2-4 people depending on roast size, or more if you use a large elk roast.

serves 4-6 | prep 10 min | cook 10 hours

Ingredients

1 roast (bear, deer, elk, or any other roasts you might have)
½ tablespoon salt
½ teaspoon pepper
½ tablespoon garlic powder
½ tablespoon onion powder
2 sprigs rosemary
2 tablespoons grass fed butter
3 cups beef broth
1 cup red wine
About 1 cup baby carrots
8-10 fingerling potatoes, various colors
8-10 mini pearl onions

Instructions

Combine the salt, pepper, onion powder and garlic powder in a bowl. Pat the roast dry then coat with the spice mixture. In a pan, heat one tablespoon of the butter over medium-high heat, then sear the roast on all sides. Remove the roast and if you want, pour a little of the red wine into the pan to deglaze it to get some extra flavor. In a crock pot, add your roast and cover with the beef broth and red wine or red wine mixture from deglazing. Add in the sprigs of rosemary and thyme. Cook on low for 10 hours. About 2 hours prior to the end of cooking, take the rest of the grass fed butter and gently sauté the carrots, potatoes, and onions for 2-3 minutes. Add them to the crockpot for the rest of the cook time.

Once finished, remove the pot roast and divide into 4 servings. Add some of the vegetables to each plate and serve.

If you want, take 1-2 cups of the pot roast liquid and set aside for gravy. Place the pot roast liquid into a pot and bring to a simmer. Allow the liquid to simmer gently until it has reduced to your desired consistency. Serve over the pot roast.

Venison Wellington

This venison wellington is a tasty take on the traditional beef wellington. The combination of the mustard, the mushroom Duxelles and the flakey puff pastry make this recipe absolutely mouth watering. This meal will serve 2-6 people depending on the size of your roast.

Venison Wellington

serves 2-6 | prep 1 hour | cook 30 min

Ingredients

2 tablespoons grass fed butter, divided
1 (3 pound) backstrap roast
Puff pastry (see sausage rolls recipe on page 21)
1 cup mushrooms, finely chopped
1 shallot, finely chopped
2 cloves garlic, finely chopped
Hot mustard
4 ounce package of prosciutto
1 egg, beaten

Instructions

Preheat the oven to 425 °F.

Remove the pastry from the refrigerator and allow to soften slightly so it can be rolled out.

Heat a cast iron skillet to medium-high heat. Melt 1 tablespoon of the butter in the cast iron, then sear the venison on all sides. Set the meat aside to cool, then baste with mustard, wrap in saran wrap, and stick in the refrigerator for about twenty minutes. While the venison is cooling, clean out the cast iron of any browned butter, then heat to medium-low heat.

Melt the second tablespoon of butter over medium-low heat, making sure the butter melts gently and does not brown. Once the butter is melted, add the shallots and garlic and begin to gently cook for about 3 minutes, softening but not browning. Add in the chopped mushrooms and gently sauté until the mushrooms are soft and have released all their liquid. Once the liquid is evaporated, remove the mixture from the heat and let cool. Lay out the pieces of prosciutto on a piece of saran wrap so that they overlap, similar to shingles on a roof, in the shape of a rectangle large enough to completely wrap around the meat. When the mushroom mixture is cool, spread it evenly over the prosciutto. Place the venison on the prosciutto and mushrooms and wrap them tightly around the meat. Wrap tightly with saran wrap and return to the fridge for another twenty minutes.

Venison Wellington

serves 2-6 | prep 1 hour | cook 30 min

Instructions Continued

Roll out the pastry into a rectangle large enough to wrap around your venison. Place your prosciutto wrapped roast directly in the center of the pastry. Next, you will want to cut the corners of the pastry so the meat is sitting in the center of a cross. To do this, cut a square from about ½ an inch from each corner of the meat. Repeat on all four corners.

Wrap the pastry around the venison, brushing any overlapping pastry with the beaten egg wash to ensure they stick together well. Once wrapped, brush more of the egg wash over the entire wellington. Gently score the top of the wellington, ensuring you do not cut completely through the pastry. If desired, lay a pastry lattice over the top and brush with egg again.

Place the wellington in the oven and set a timer for about 20 minutes. After 20 minutes, check the internal temperature of the meat. Increase the time by 5 minute increments until the meat reaches about 125 °F. If the pastry begins to darken too much, place a layer of foil over the top to prevent it from burning while the meat reaches temperature. Once the wellington is cooked, remove it from the oven and let rest for at least 10 minutes.

To serve, cut into ¾" slices and serve with mashed potatoes and gravy.

Wild Turkey

Wild Turkey Enchiladas

Wild Turkey Noodle Soup

Parmesan Crusted Turkey Breasts

Wild Turkey and Rice Soup

Wild Turkey Piccata

Wild Turkey Pot Pie

Wild Turkey Enchiladas

Wild Turkey Enchiladas

serves 10 | pre cook 8 hours | prep 30 min | cook 45 min

Ingredients

1 wild turkey breast and 1 leg
1 tablespoon olive oil
1 small onion, chopped
2 cloves garlic, minced
½ tablespoon chili powder
1 tablespoon cumin
½ teaspoon paprika
½ teaspoon salt
½ teaspoon pepper
Cayenne pepper to taste
1 (4 ounce) can green chiles
16 ounces salsa verde
16 ounces sour cream
4 cups Mexican blend cheese
10 inch flour tortillas

Instructions

In the morning, add your turkey meat into a crockpot, cover with chicken or turkey stock, and cook on low for 8 hours.

Preheat your oven to 350 °F. Remove the turkey from the crockpot and allow to cool. Remove the leg meat from the bone, then chop all the meat into bite sized pieces and place in a large mixing bowl. In a large frying pan, heat the olive oil over medium-high heat. Sauté the onions until they are translucent, then add the green chiles and cook for 1 minute more. Remove them from the heat and add to the mixing bowl with the turkey. In a separate bowl, combine the salsa verde, sour cream, and seasonings to create your sauce. Take about ¼ cup of this sauce and use it to coat the bottom of a 9"x13" baking dish, then add another ½ cup or so to the turkey mixture.

Take one tortilla and spoon a generous amount of the turkey mixture along the middle, sprinkle with cheese, then roll into an enchilada. Place your enchilada into the baking dish and repeat with the remaining ingredients. Once you've rolled all your enchiladas, coat them with the remaining sauce, then top with the rest of the cheese. Bake for about 45 minutes to an hour, until the cheese has melted and starts to bubble.

Wild Turkey Noodle Soup

Wild Turkey Noodle Soup

serves 6 | pre cook 8 hours | prep 10 min | cook 1 hour

Ingredients

1 wild turkey breast
3 cups turkey or chicken stock
1 tablespoon olive oil
1 clove garlic
¼ onion
1 cup carrots, sliced
1 cup celery, sliced
64 ounces turkey or chicken broth
¼ teaspoon celery salt
¼ teaspoon salt
¼ teaspoon pepper
½ package egg noodles

Instructions

Place the turkey breast in a crock pot and cover with chicken or turkey stock. Cook on low for 8 hours. Once done, shred the turkey into bite size pieces and set aside.

In a large pot, heat the olive oil over medium-high heat. Sauté the garlic, onion, carrots and celery until soft. Add in the broth, turkey, both salts and the pepper and bring the soup to a boil. Turn the heat down to medium-low and simmer for about 1 hour. Add in the egg noodles and cook another 10 minutes or until the noodles are cooked through. If you plan to freeze or refrigerate the soup, do not add the noodles and instead, add them in when you reheat the soup.

Parmesan Crusted Turkey Breast

Parmesan Crusted Turkey Breast

serves 2 | prep 10 min | cook 30 min

Ingredients

2 wild turkey breasts
½ cup breadcrumbs
½ cup grated parmesan cheese
2 eggs
1 teaspoon salt
1 teaspoon pepper
1 teaspoon paprika
¼ cup vegetable oil

Instructions

Using a meat tenderizer (or rolling pin if you don't have one), pound the turkey breasts so they are a uniform ½" thickness. Pat each turkey breast dry and set aside. Grab two wide and shallow bowls and place them next to each other. In the first bowl, crack the eggs and beat completely. In the second bowl, combine the breadcrumbs, parmesan cheese, salt, pepper and paprika. Dip each turkey breast into the egg mixture, then into the breadcrumb mixture, coating completely. Repeat a second time if the turkey breasts aren't completely coated.

Coat the bottom of a large frying pan with vegetable oil and heat over high heat. Once the oil reaches temperature, place each turkey breast into the hot oil and cook for 3-4 minutes per side, or until the breadcrumbs on each side are golden brown. When the turkey breasts are nearly done, sprinkle some freshly grated parmesan over the top and allow it to melt. Serve with your favorite pasta dish or with a side of roasted vegetables.

Wild Turkey and Rice Soup

Wild Turkey and Rice Soup

serves 6 | pre cook 8 hours | prep 10 min | cook 1 hour

Ingredients

1 wild turkey leg or breast
3 cups turkey or chicken stock
1 tablespoon olive oil
½ an onion
1 clove garlic, minced
1 small red bell pepper
64 ounces turkey or chicken broth
1 cup wild rice
¼ teaspoon chili flakes
½ teaspoon salt
½ teaspoon pepper

Instructions

In the morning, place the turkey in a crock pot and cover with chicken broth. Cook on low for 8 hours. Once cooked, remove the turkey from the crockpot and shred into bite sized pieces then set aside.

In a large pot, heat the olive oil over medium heat. Add the garlic, onion and bell pepper and sauté until the onions are translucent. Add in the broth, wild turkey, and spices. Bring to a gentle boil, then add in the rice. Turn the heat down to medium-low and simmer for 1 hour.

Wild Turkey Piccata

Wild Turkey Piccata

serves 2-4 | prep 30 min | cook 15 min

Ingredients

1 wild turkey breast
½ pound angel hair pasta
½ cup flour
½ teaspoon salt
¼ teaspoon pepper
¼ cup olive oil
¼ cup of butter
½ a shallot, finely chopped
2 cloves garlic, finely chopped
1 tablespoon flour
½ cup chicken broth
¼ cup white wine
¼ cup fresh lemon juice
¼ cup heavy whipping cream
¼ cup capers
1 tablespoon chopped parsley
leaves, for garnish

Instructions

Butterfly the turkey breast by cutting it in half horizontally, making two cutlets. Turkey breasts tend to be quite big, so if necessary, cut each cutlet in half to make four equal serving sizes. Place each of the turkey cutlets on a cutting board and cover with saran wrap. Take a meat tenderizer (or rolling pin if you don't have one) and pound the turkey so it is about ¼" thick.

Cook the angel hair pasta according to the package instructions and set aside when done.

While the pasta is cooking, mix the flour, salt, and pepper together and place on a plate next to your stove. In a large pan, heat the olive oil over medium-high heat. Once the oil reaches temperature, take one cutlet and dredge it in flour, covering it completely. Tap off the excess and place in the frying pan. Repeat with a second cutlet. Cook the turkey for about 3-4 minutes per side, or until golden brown. Check the internal temperature of the turkey to make sure it is around 165 °F. Place the cooked turkey breast on a plate in a warm oven while you repeat the process with the remaining cutlets.

In another pan, melt the butter over medium heat. Once melted, add the garlic and shallots to the butter and gently sauté until soft. Add in the flour and mix completely. Once the flour is combined with the butter, slowly whisk in the chicken broth, white wine and lemon juice. Bring the mixture to a gentle boil, then turn the heat down and simmer until the sauce is slightly reduced. Whisk in the capers and heavy cream, and keep the sauce on low until ready to serve. Serve the turkey over the pasta and cover with the creamy sauce. Garnish with parsley.

Wild Turkey Pot Pie

Wild Turkey Pot Pie

This recipe is my favorite way to eat wild turkey and it also serves as a great way to use up any vegetables you have kicking around in your fridge. Some other veggies you can add are mushrooms, broccoli or even Brussels sprouts. Because there is so much flavor in this dish, it's great for any upland bird, not just turkey, and also works great with chicken.

serves 6-8 | pre cook 8 hours | prep 20 min | cook 40 min

Ingredients

For the Turkey
1 wild turkey breast and 1 leg
4 cups turkey or chicken stock

For the Crust
12 ounces flour, sifted
6 ounces bear lard
½ cup ice water
Dash of salt

For the Filling
2 tablespoons butter
2 tablespoons flour
1 cup milk
1 cup chicken/turkey broth
(you can use the liquid from the crock pot for this)
1 cup carrots, chopped
1 cup celery, chopped
½ cup peas
Cooked turkey meat, chopped

Instructions

To cook the turkey: In the morning, put the turkey into a crockpot, cover with chicken or turkey stock and cook on low for 8 hours. For this recipe, I usually use one turkey breast and one turkey leg, giving me a mixture of light and dark meat, but you can use whatever turkey meat you have.

To make the crust: Sift the flour into a large mixing bowl. Cut the bear lard into ½" cubes, then begin mixing in with the flour using a spatula. If the bear lard begins to liquefy, put the mixture in the fridge for a couple minutes, then continue the process. Begin slowly adding the ice water, mixing regularly until you have a sturdy dough. Refrigerate for 10 minutes before rolling out. To roll out, take half the dough and roll into a ball. Place the ball of dough between two sheets of parchment paper and roll into a flat circle, about a ¼" thick. Repeat with the other half of the dough to make two equal pie crusts. Refrigerate.

Wild Turkey Pot Pie

Instructions Continued

To make the filling: In a small saucepan, melt the butter over medium heat, then whisk in the flour. Once the flour and butter are combined, slowly add in the milk and chicken broth, whisking constantly. Once all liquid is added, turn the heat down to low and simmer until the sauce reaches your desired thickness (some prefer thicker, some more soupy). At this point, combine the vegetables, turkey meat and gravy in a mixing bowl. You can add as little or as much of the gravy as you want depending on how soupy you want your pie to be.

In a pie plate, lay one of the chilled pie crusts down and push it into the edges of the plate. Pour in the filling mixture and smooth out, then lay the second pie crust over the top. Crimp the sides using your fingers or a fork, then make some small slits in the center of the pie to let the steam out. Cook in a 400 °F oven until the crust is golden brown, about 40 minutes. Serve hot and top with some of the leftover gravy if desired.

Bear

Bear Stroganoff

Crispy Bear Carnitas

BBQ Pulled Bear Sandwich

Bear Stroganoff

serves 2-4 | prep 10 min | cook 20 min

Ingredients

1 pound bear backstrap
¼ cup flour
4 tablespoons grass fed butter
1 clove garlic, minced
½ an onion, chopped
5 cremini mushrooms, sliced
1 cup beef broth
1 tablespoon tomato paste
2 cups sour cream
1 package of egg noodles

Instructions

Cut the backstrap into thin, bite size pieces. If necessary, partially freeze the meat to make it easier to cut. Pat the meat dry, then coat the pieces with half of the flour. In a cast iron skillet, heat 2 tablespoons of the butter over medium-high heat and add in the meat. Brown the meat on all sides, making sure there is no pink left (you want to make sure to thoroughly cook bear meat, see note). Add in the garlic, onion and mushrooms, cooking them until they're soft. Lower the heat to medium, then add the remaining butter. Stir the flour into the melted butter. Slowly stir in the beef broth, whisking it into the butter/flour mixture until it creates a sauce. Whisk in the tomato paste and sour cream and combine all ingredients thoroughly. Simmer until the sauce has thickened, about five minutes. While simmering, cook the noodles according to their package instructions. Serve the sauce over the noodles and enjoy.

Note:

Bears are known carriers of the trichinella parasite, which is responsible for causing trichinosis. Although this particular parasite can die at 137 °F, the possibility for human error while reading internal meat temperatures, combined with discrepancies from cheap thermometers, has led the USDA to recommend a minimum internal cooking temperature of 160 °F. Although some strains of trichinella can be killed by prolonged freezing, the strains that commonly infect bears can not. It is best to cook the meat more well done to avoid any potential illness.

Crispy Bear Carnitas

Crispy Bear Carnitas

If someone tells you they don't like bear, make them this recipe and dare them to not enjoy it. These bear carnitas are by far my favorite way to eat bear meat. They have so much flavor from the slow cooking, and frying the meat afterwards gives them a delicious crunch. This meal makes an appearance in our house nearly every week and as a bonus, if you have a larger bear roast, you can save half of it before the frying stage and use in our pulled bear sandwiches on page 85 (though we almost never make it that far because we can't help but eat it all as carnitas).

serves 2-4 | pre cook 6-8 hours | prep 10 min | cook 10 min

Ingredients

1 pound bear roast
1 bottle of citrus IPA beer
1 clove garlic, chopped
½ small onion, chopped
½ teaspoon salt
½ teaspoon pepper
3 tablespoons olive oil
1 tablespoon chili powder
½ tablespoon cumin
½ teaspoon paprika
Dash of cayenne pepper to taste
Small corn or flour tortillas
Choice of toppings

Instructions

In a crockpot, add the bear roast, garlic, onion, salt and pepper. Pour in the citrus IPA, making sure to cover at least half of the roast. Cook on low for 6-8 hours.

Once the meat has finished cooking, remove it from the crockpot and shred it with a fork. Pour about 3 tablespoons of olive oil into a frying pan over medium-high heat. Add the shredded bear and begin to fry it. After about 2 minutes, add the chili powder, cumin, paprika and cayenne pepper. Fry until the meat is crispy on the outside but still juicy and tender on the inside, about 7-10 minutes. This gives your carnitas a delicious crunch.

I like to serve these with corn tortillas, chopped cilantro, diced tomatoes, sour cream and your favorite cheese. Finally, squeeze ¼ of a lime over the top of your carnitas and enjoy.

For a low carb option, skip the tortillas and serve over a bed of lettuce.

BBQ Pulled Bear Sandwich

BBQ Pulled Bear Sandwich

serves 2-4 | prep 10 min | cook 8 hours

Ingredients

1 pound bear roast
½ teaspoon garlic powder
½ teaspoon onion powder
1 teaspoon salt
1 teaspoon pepper
1 citrus IPA

Instructions

Place the roast in your crockpot and cover with your favorite beer. I like to use a citrus IPA because it gives the meat a really great flavor, but you can use any beer you like. Add the garlic, onion, salt and pepper and set your crockpot to cook low for 8 hours.

Once the meat is cooked, remove it from the crock pot and shred it with a fork. Add in your favorite barbecue sauce and serve over a brioche bun, topped with coleslaw.

A low carb option for serving pulled bear is in a lettuce boat. I take one romaine leaf, place the pulled bear inside the leaf (like a boat) and drizzle some Wilderness Kitchen barbecue sauce over the top.

Wilderness Kitchen Barbecue Sauce

In a large pan, combine 2 cups ketchup, ½ cup brown sugar, 1 cup pineapple juice, 2 tablespoons white vinegar, 1 tablespoon Worcestershire sauce, 1 tablespoon soy sauce, 1 tablespoon molasses, 1 ½ teaspoon salt, ½ teaspoon garlic powder, ½ teaspoon onion powder, ½ teaspoon paprika, ½ teaspoon chipotle powder, ¼ tsp pepper and ¼ tsp cayenne pepper. Mix all ingredients thoroughly and bring to a gentle boil. Turn the heat down to low and simmer for at least an hour. Either serve immediately or transfer to a mason jar and use or freeze within a week.

Crab Cakes

Crab Cakes

One of my favorite summer pastimes is crabbing in the Puget Sound. I spend many days every year at my mom's house crabbing in the sunshine and when the fishing is good, I'll whip up a huge batch of crab cakes for friends and family. They are a crowd pleaser and relatively easy to make. I like to serve them with a siracha-mayo dipping sauce that has just the right amount of kick.

serves 4 | prep 30 min | cook 10 min

Ingredients

½ pound crab meat
¼ cup green onions, diced
¼ cup bell peppers, chopped
¼ cup cilantro, chopped
1 cup panko bread crumbs
(more for forming the cakes)
1 cup mayo
Salt and pepper to taste

Note:

For the dipping sauce, combine ¼ cup mayonnaise with ½ tablespoon Siracha in a small bowl

Instructions

In a large mixing bowl, combine all ingredients and mix well. Test out making a crab cake by grabbing a spoonful of the mixture and trying to form it into a puck. If it doesn't stick together and crumbles, add more mayonnaise; if it is too gooey and falls apart, add more breadcrumbs. The key is creating a perfect consistency so the crab cakes stick together nicely.

When packing the crab cakes, take a large spoonful of the mixture and tightly form a ball. Squish the ball down into a disk shape, then square off the edges making an even, hockey puck shape. Make sure your crab cakes are tightly packed or they will fall apart while cooking. Coat the outside of each crab cake in breadcrumbs.

In a large frying pan, coat the bottom generously with vegetable oil and heat over medium-high heat. Place each crab cake gently in the oil and cook until the bottom is golden brown, then carefully flip and cook the other side the same. Serve immediately with the siracha-mayo dipping sauce.

Made in United States
Troutdale, OR
12/06/2023

15284050R00052